Collins

INTERNATIONAL
PRIMARY
GLOBAL
PERSPECTIVES

KU-738-825

Student's Book 2

William Collins' dream of knowledge for all began with the publication of his first book in 1819.

A self-educated mill worker, he not only enriched millions of lives, but also founded a flourishing publishing house. Today, staying true to this spirit, Collins books are packed with inspiration, innovation and practical expertise.

They place you at the centre of a world of possibility and give you exactly what you need to explore it.

Collins. Freedom to teach.

Published by Collins

An imprint of HarperCollins*Publishers*
The News Building, 1 London Bridge Street, London, SE1 9GF, UK

HarperCollins*Publishers*
Macken House, 39/40 Mayor Street Upper, Dublin 1 D01 C9W8

Browse the complete Collins catalogue at
collins.co.uk

© HarperCollins*Publishers* Limited 2023

10 9 8 7 6 5 4 3 2 1

ISBN 978-0-00-854955-8

All rights reserved. No part of this publication may be reproduced, stored in a retrieval system, or transmitted in any form or by any means, electronic, mechanical, photocopying, recording or otherwise, without the prior written permission of the Publisher or a licence permitting restricted copying in the United Kingdom issued by the Copyright Licensing Agency Ltd, 5th Floor, Shackleton House, 4 Battle Bridge Lane, London SE1 2HX.

British Library Cataloguing-in-Publication Data
A catalogue record for this publication is available from the British Library.

Cambridge International copyright material in this publication is reproduced under licence and remains the intellectual property of Cambridge Assessment International Education.

Third-party websites and resources referred to in this publication have not been endorsed by Cambridge Assessment International Education.

Endorsement indicates that a resource has passed Cambridge International's rigorous quality-assurance process and is suitable to support the delivery of a Cambridge International curriculum framework. However, endorsed resources are not the only suitable materials available to support teaching and learning, and are not essential to be used to achieve the qualification. Resource lists found on the Cambridge International website will include this resource and other endorsed resources.

Any example answers to questions taken from past question papers, practice questions, accompanying marks and mark schemes included in this resource have been written by the authors and are for guidance only. They do not replicate examination papers.

In examinations the way marks are awarded may be different. Any references to assessment and/or assessment preparation are the publisher's interpretation of the curriculum framework requirements. Examiners will not use endorsed resources as a source of material for any assessment set by Cambridge International.

While the publishers have made every attempt to ensure that advice on the qualification and its assessment is accurate, the official curriculum framework, specimen assessment materials and any associated assessment guidance materials produced by the awarding body are the only authoritative source of information and should always be referred to for definitive guidance. Cambridge International recommends that teachers consider using a range of teaching and learning resources based on their own professional judgement of their students' needs.

Cambridge International has not paid for the production of this resource, nor does Cambridge International receive any royalties from its sale. For more information about the endorsement process, please visit www.cambridgeinternational.org/endorsed-resources

Series editor: Nick Coates
Author: Daphne Paizee, Sula Delafuente, Fiona Macgregor
Publisher: Elaine Higgleton
Product developer: Roisin Leahy
Development editor: Lucy Cooper
Copyeditor: Catherine Dakin
Proofreader: Gudrun Kaiser
Illustrations: Jouve India Ltd.
Text permissions researcher: Rachel Thorne
Cover designer: Gordon MacGilp
Typesetter: David Jimenez, Ken Vail Graphic Design
Production controller: Lyndsey Rogers
Printed in the UK by Martins the Printers

We are grateful to MInal Mistry for providing feedback on the Student's Book as it was developed.

MIX
Paper | Supporting responsible forestry
FSC™ C007454

This book is produced from independently certified FSC™ paper to ensure responsible forest management.

For more information visit: harpercollins.co.uk/green

Contents

How to use this book

Use this book in your lessons, to learn about a range of global topics!

The skills box shows you the main and subsidiary skills that you will learn and practise in this lesson.

> ✓ **Main**
> ✓ Subsidiary

> **Key terms**
>
> **Key terms** are important words or phrases that will help you to understand what to do in each lesson.

> **Useful language**
>
> *The useful phrases and sentences provided will help you to discuss the topic …*

📖 An activity that involves reading

👂 An activity that involves listening

👥 An activity that involves working in a pair

👥 An activity that involves working in a group

> **Talking point**
>
> - Look back on what you have learned in the lesson, and talk about things that went well with your classmates.

> **Before you go**
>
> - Think about how you will use your new skills!

Unit 1 Talking technology

What do you know?
- What is technology?
- How do we use technology?
- Technology then and now
- Can we use technology to play together?
- Technology and games
- Which game shall we play?

In this unit, you will:
- talk about technology and devices we use
- design a digital game and talk about how to play it.

1.1 What is technology?

1 😊 📖 💬 **Look at the pictures and answer the questions.**

- What is Aimee doing?
- What is she playing with?

Aimee is playing a game on her tablet.

What does it do?

Aimee thinks.

Aimee checks with Mama. Mama helps her.

2 😊 💬 **Listen to the story and answer the questions.**

Why did Aimee need help?

Did Aimee do the right thing? Why?

3 😊 💬 **Do you use technology? What devices do you use?**

Play the game 'What am I thinking of?'

Do you have a **device** at home?

2

> Where do you see it?

> Who uses it?

Key terms

technology: the use of knowledge to invent new devices or tools

problem: a situation that causes difficulties

device: something that is mechanical or electrical (such as a phone or a television) that we use for a particular purpose

4 👥 💬 **Choose a device that you use at school or at home.**

a Use the worksheet to help you prepare to talk about your device.

b Show your picture to the class and let them ask you questions about it.

Useful language

Listen carefully when someone asks you a question so that you can give them the information they are looking for. For example:

Question	Answer
What do you use the device for?	*We use the device for/to …*
How does it work?	*It works with a battery, or ...*
How does it help you?	*It is useful because …* *It helps us to …*

Talking point

- Did you find it useful playing 'What am I thinking of?' to help you prepare to talk about your chosen device?

Before you go

- Can devices help us to learn?

1.2 How do we use technology?

1 🁢 🗨 **Name the device in each picture. Where do we use them?**

A

B

C

D

E

F

2 🁢 🗨 **Look at this diagram. Compare it with the pictures in Activity 1.**

- What does the diagram show us?
- What more does it tell us than the pictures in Activity 1?

3 🁢 ✏ **Discuss how you use technology in your own home. Draw a picture diagram to show your ideas. Use the worksheet.**

Living room   Bedroom

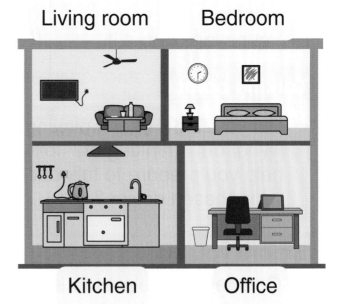

Kitchen   Office

4 👥 💬 **Read the information in this ideas map. Ask each other questions to understand how the map works.**

What information does this **ideas map** give us?

Why are there different colours in the ideas map?

Why are there arrows?

Microwave: to heat our food

Kettle: to boil water

Electric toothbrush: to clean our teeth

Technology in the house

Television: to watch the news

Clock: to tell the time

Lamp: to help us read

5 👥 ✏️ **Draw an ideas map that gives more information about technology that you use at home. Use the worksheet.**

How can you use colours and arrows to make the information clearer?

6 👥 💬 **Present your ideas map to the class. Explain what it shows.**

Key term

ideas map: a graphic diagram to help us show and sort out ideas

Talking point

• What can you use an ideas map for? Share your ideas.

Before you go

• Which technology device in your home do you use the most? Why?

1.3 Technology then and now

✓ **Communication**
✓ Evaluation
✓ Research

1 👥 👂 **Look at the pictures. Listen to the story. Who is it about? What are they talking about?**

Our schools

1

> When did you go to school?

> Before you were born, Tenda!

2

> My teacher used chalk to write on a blackboard. We used pencils and paper.

3

> We sat in rows at desks.

4

> My teacher used an overhead projector.

5

> What's that?

> It was a device that we used to read together.

6

> We also read in class. We read books or we use tablets.

7

> My classroom is very different!

8

> We have a smart board.

9

> I need to visit your school!

2 Compare the schools in the story.

  a Complete the diagram with your teacher.
  - What tools or devices did grandmother use?
  - What tools or devices does Tenda use?
  - What did they learn at school?

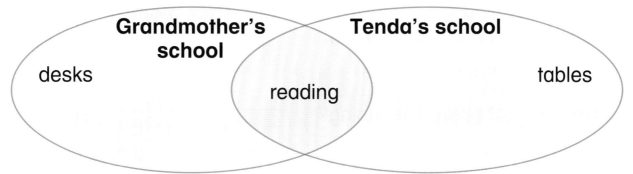

Grandmother's school | reading | Tenda's school
desks | | tables

  b Which tools or devices do you think work best? Why?

3 Compare your school with the school in the story. Use the worksheet.

4 Draw a picture of something else that helps you to learn. Choose some of these questions to help you.

What does it look like?   Why is it big or small?

Why do you like it?   How can it help you to learn?

I can use it to read because ...

Talking point

- Did you give good reasons for your ideas today? Write your answers in a table like this.

My ideas	My reasons

Before you go

- Why do we learn about things in the past?

1.4 Can we use technology to play together?

1 👥 💬 **Look at the pictures carefully. Then close your books and talk about them.**

Ask each other questions.

> What are they doing?

> Who is using technology to play?

> Where are they playing?

2 🤝 💬 ✏️ **Prepare questions for a survey.**

- What is the most popular game in your class?
- Does it use technology?
- Talk about this with your partner.
- Write down questions you could ask your classmates to find out which is the most popular game. Use the worksheet.

Useful language

What is …?
Where do you …?
What do you use to …?
Is … ?

3 🤝 👥 💬 **Ask students from another class your questions.**

a Which questions gave you the information you were looking for?

b Tick the two best questions on the worksheet.

4 🤝 💬 ✏️ **Do a survey with your two best questions. Record the answers on the worksheet.**

5 🤝 👥 💬 **What did you find out? Share your results with the class.**

So what do you think of this game?

Well, first of all, I think that, and then …. And then … and so … because …

Talking point

- Which questions gave you the best answers? Why did some questions not work? Can you think of better questions now?

Before you go

- Do the students in your class enjoy using technology to play games with others?

1.5 Technology and games

1 **Look at these pictures.**

> Do you know any of these games?

> Do you play them in groups or alone?

> What do you need to play the games?

2   **Read about the games.**

Game 1 Mbube Mbube (from South Africa)

Everyone stands in a circle.

Someone is the lion, and someone is the impala.

The lion and impala put on blindfolds. Someone spins them both around.

The lion tries to catch the impala.

When the lion gets close, everyone shouts: 'Mbube! Mbube!' loudly.

When the lion is not close, everyone says: 'Mbube Mbube' quietly.

Game 2 I like coffee (from the USA)

Two people turn a skipping rope.

One person jumps over the rope as it turns.

Everyone says:

I like coffee.

And I like tea.

The person who is jumping says:

I want … (Say a name.)

To jump with me!

They jump together. The first person jumps out and the game continues.

Game 3 Jungle playhouse

This is an **app** so you need a mobile phone to play this game.

Tap on the picture on the **screen** to start.

Go to different places and meet new animals.

You can do different things in each place. You can look after a sick animal or look for an animal who is hiding.

3 👥 👥 💬 **Talk about the games. Use these questions to help you.**

What game uses a device?

Which games do not use a device?

Which game would you most like to play? Why?

How can you learn to play these games?

4 👥 💬 **Think of a game that you can play. Tell your partner about it. Ask each other questions.**

- Do you need a device to play this game?
- How do you play the game?

Key terms

screen: the flat part on a device on which you can read and see things

app: a program with a picture on a phone, tablet or computer, which allows you to do special things

Useful language

I like …
You can play …
You use a …
You tap on …
You score points for …

Talking point

- What questions did you ask about the games?
- Why is it important to listen? What can help you to listen?

Before you go

- What can happen if we don't listen carefully? Can you think of a problem you could have if you haven't listened properly?

11

1.6 Which game shall we play?

✓ Collaboration
✓ Reflection

1 👥 💬 **What do you need to do to work well in a team?**

Choose ideas from these cards, that you think are important for teamwork. Then compare the ideas that you chose.

| listen well | be clever | respect others |

| work quickly | be patient | trust others |

> Which idea is the most important for you? Why?

> Which idea is the least important? Why?

2 👥 💬 **Talk about the games in the pictures.**

- Which games will you play on a mobile phone?
- Which games have characters, like in stories?
- Which games have adventures?
- Which games are puzzles?
- What sounds will you hear if you play the games?
- How will you know when the game is finished?
- Do you play these games alone or in groups?

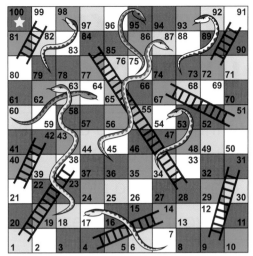

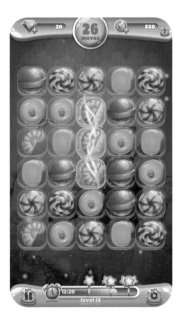

3 👥 💬 ✏️ **Design a game. Use the worksheet and work through the steps.**

> You will need to share ideas to work as a team.

4 👥 💬 ✏️ **Discuss how you play the game. Write instructions on the worksheet.**

Talking point

- What did you do to help your team today?
- Talk about one person in your team and how they helped to design the game.

Before you go

- What could you do to make your game better?

Unit 1 Final task: Share your game!

What?	Think about the game you designed in the last lesson. How can you make it better?
	Explain to others how to play your game.
	Ask people in your class questions about their games.
	Think about what went well in your presentation.
How?	Work in the same groups as the last lesson.

1 👥 🗣 **What do you think you need to do to be successful in this task? Listen to your teacher.**

Success means ...
We have worked together to make a game that will be fun to play.
Everyone will be able to play this game.
Our game has clear rules and everyone understands what to do.

2 🏃 💬 **In your team, talk about the game you designed in Lesson 1.6.**

a Answer these questions.
- How can you make it better?
- How will you present your game to the class? Will you make a poster or present it on a screen?
- Do you have everything you need to do this?
- Will you take turns to speak? What will each person say?
- What questions will you need to answer?

b Prepare your presentations.

c What will you do to be successful?

3 🏃 💬 **Present your game idea to the class.**

Follow these steps:
- Say what kind of game it is. Show your picture.
- Explain how the game works.
- End with a short conclusion.
- Answer questions from the rest of the class.

4 🏃 💬 ✏️ **Talk about the games presented and answer these questions.**

a Which games did you like the most?

b Was any game similar to your game?

c What ideas can you use to improve your own game?

5 👤 ✏️ **What part did you play in this task? What did you do well?**

Reflection: How successful was your presentation?

a 👥💬 Discuss the task in your group.

Final task checklist			
Did you all help to present the game?	☺	😐	☹
Did you listen to each other and discuss the ideas?	☺	😐	☹
Did the other groups find your presentation interesting?	☺	😐	☹

b 👤✏️ Complete the worksheet.

c 👥💬 Discuss the presentations with your teacher.

- Which presentations worked well?
- Why did they work well?
- What could you have done differently?

Before you go

- What other games would you like to know more about?
- Would you like to learn how to use coding in order to make a game?

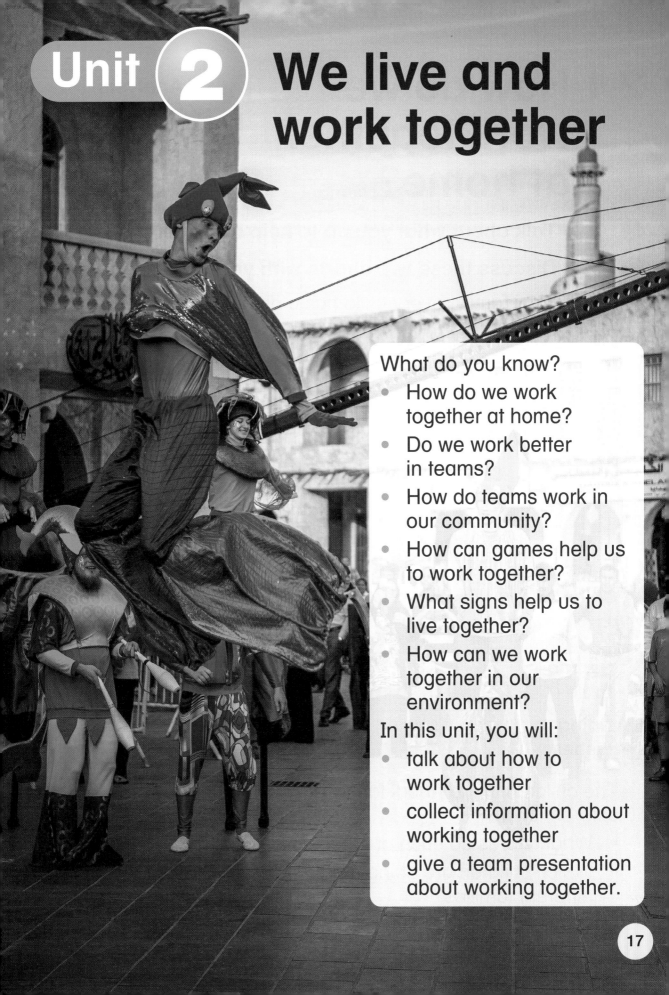

Unit **2** We live and work together

What do you know?
- How do we work together at home?
- Do we work better in teams?
- How do teams work in our community?
- How can games help us to work together?
- What signs help us to live together?
- How can we work together in our environment?

In this unit, you will:
- talk about how to work together
- collect information about working together
- give a team presentation about working together.

2.1 How do we work together at home?

✓ Analysis
✓ Communication

① 👥 💬 **Talk about what you do to help at home.**

② 👥 💬 **Discuss these two charts with your partner.**

In the Patel family, every child has a dinnertime chore. This is the chart that Mrs Patel has on her fridge.

Chart 1 The Patel family

Dinnertime chores for the children	
Set the table	Amit
Clear the table	Priti
Wash the dishes	Ratnesh
Dry the dishes	Manish

Chart 2 The Abadi family's dinnertime chores

	Monday	Tuesday	Wednesday	Thursday	Friday
Setting table	Sami	Shamila	Sami	Shamila	Sami
Doing dishes	Shamila	Sami	Shamila	Sami	Shamila

The children in the Abadi family also help. But they have a different chart.

- What chores do each of these children have?
- Which children are doing the same chores in the two different families?

18

- Why do you think Sami and Shamila help more than the children in Chart 1?
- Why should we help each other?

3 👥 💬 **Talk to your partner about how you can help at home.**

> What do you help with at home?

> I wash the dishes.

> How often?

> Does anyone help you?

- Do you have chores to do every day? What are they?
- What other chore could you do to help?
- How would this make your grown-ups feel?

4 👥 🧑 ✏️ **Complete the worksheet about how you can help at home.**

Talking point
- What happens if you don't help at home?

Before you go
- Write down three new things that you will do to help at home. Take your list to your grown-ups at home. And then *do* those three things!

2.2 Do we work better in teams?

✓ Collaboration
✓ Research

1  **Ask ten people this question.**

> Do you like working in a team, or do you like working alone?

> I like working in a team. It's more fun.

> I like working alone because teams can make a lot of noise.

- First write down the two options in the question:
  - I like working in a team.
  - I like working alone.
- Then ask ten students your question. Make a tick mark next to the option when you get the answer from someone.
- Next, use your information to fill in the **bar chart** on the worksheet. Colour one block on the bar chart for each answer you get.

Key term

bar chart: a graph that looks like a lot of bars put next to each other. Each block in one bar represents one item. Here is an example. Each block represents one person who likes that sport. How many people like each sport?

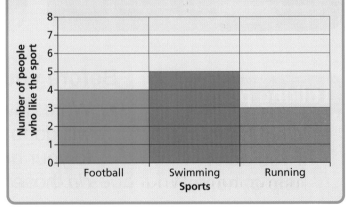

2 👥 💬 **Look at the pictures and discuss how these teams work together.**

- What is each team doing?
- What is each person in the team doing?
- Are some people doing the same thing? Why?
- How does the action of each person make the team work?
- Why is teamwork important in these jobs?

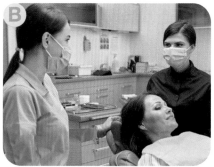

3 👥 💬 **Try some teamwork. Build a spaghetti tower in teams. Listen carefully to the instructions from your teacher.**

You have three minutes. Go!

- How well did your team work together?
- What could your team have done to work together better?
- Did you enjoy working in a team? Give a reason for your answer.

Talking point

- What makes a good team?

Before you go

- Make a class graph about who likes working alone and who likes working in a team. Follow your teacher's instructions. What does your class graph show?

2.3 How do teams work in our community?

1 😃 💬 👂 **What is this story about?**

Keeping the streets clean

We are the team who collects your waste.

I am the driver.

I blow my whistle when we must stop.

I collect the bin and put it on the truck.

We take turns to blow the whistle. We take turns to collect the bins.

We are a good team.

Discuss these questions about the story with your partner.

- How many people are in this team?
- What does the team do?
- How do they share the work?

22

2 What teams work in our community?

- Talk about the teams that work at your school, for example, in the canteen or library.
- Which teams work in your neighbourhood, for example, keeping the street clean?
- How else can you find out about teamwork in your **community**?

3 Write three questions about one of the teams who help us. Use the worksheet.

Think about what each team member does.

Then think about how each member's job helps the team.

- Choose one person to interview about the team.
- Write their answers on the worksheet.
- Keep your **data** for the final task at the end of the unit.

Key terms

community: a group of people who live in a particular place, or who are similar in some way

data: information, especially when it is in the form of facts or statistics (numbers)

Talking point

- Share your questions and answers. Who has similar information? Is anything very interesting?
- What did you learn while doing Activity 3? What was difficult about this task?

Before you go

- Which team would you like to join in your community?

2.4 How can games help us to work together?

1 👥 💬 **Do you like team games?**

2 👥 💬 **Look at the pictures and talk about the games.**

- Do you know what each game is called?
- How many people play the game?
- What is the aim of the game?
- Do the players need any equipment to play the game?

3 👥 💬 **Look at the pictures and answer the questions.**

What is the aim of the game?

What do the team players need to do to win?

Does it help to have someone leading the team?

What happens if the team don't all pull together?

4 👥 💬 **Play the games with your class.**

5 👥 💬 ✏️ **Which games made you all work together?**

- Were these games good for teamwork? Why, or why not?
- Which game was not good for teamwork?
- Do a survey and fill in your results on the worksheet.

Talking point

- What team game did you enjoy? What did you learn about teams by playing it?

Before you go

- Talk about other team games with your partner. What games do you and your family play?

2.5 What signs help us to live together?

1 👥 💬 **Have you seen these signs? Answer the questions.**

- What do these signs mean?
- Where have you seen these signs?
- Why were the signs put in those places?
- What would happen if there were no signs like these?

Key term

pictogram: a simple drawing that represents something

2 👥 💬 **Look at the pictogram.**

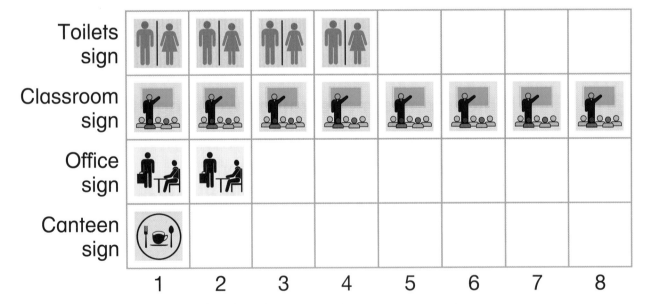

	1	2	3	4	5	6	7	8
Toilets sign	●	●	●	●				
Classroom sign	●	●	●	●	●	●	●	●
Office sign	●	●						
Canteen sign	●							

This **pictogram** was made by students, who counted and recorded the number of signs they saw. Ask each other questions about the pictogram.

26

> What do these signs mean?

> How many classrooms are in this school?

3 👥 ✏️ Find and count the signs at your school.

- Walk around the school and the school grounds with your partner.
- Write down or draw at least five signs that you see.
- If there is more than one of the same kind of sign, make a mark for each one you see.

For example:

Toilet	II
Don't run	IIII
Exit	II

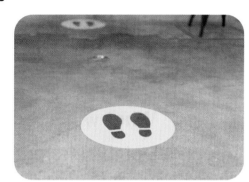

4 👥 ✏️ Make a pictogram

- Now, use the information you have found to make a pictogram.
- Record the signs you found on the worksheet.
- Draw a picture of each kind of sign in the first column. Then draw signs going along the row, according to the number of the signs you saw.

Talking point

- What was challenging about this research and making your pictogram? Did you and your partner share the work?

Before you go

Talk about your research.

- What signs did you find that help us to live and work together?
- How do these signs help us?

2.6 How can we work together in our environment?

✓ **Collaboration**
✓ Reflection

1 👥 💬 **Prepare for your trip.**

- Divide into teams.
- Discuss what you will need.

2 👥 ✏️ **What will your team do?**

> **Key term**
> **litter:** rubbish that is left lying around outside

- Look at the photographs and the captions.
- Decide what your team will do.
- Write down your goal at the top of the worksheet.

Our team will pick up **litter**.

We will sweep the leaves.

We will put in plants.

We will water the plants.

3 👥 💬 **Work in your teams. Complete your task.**

4 👥 👤 💬 ✏️ **Report back to the class.**

- How well did your team work together on your task?
- What was easy?
- What was difficult?
- Did you do what you planned to do?
- What did you learn from this activity?
- If you did this activity again, what would you do differently?

Now complete the worksheet.

Talking point
- What did you learn from doing this activity?

Before you go
- What can you do to continue this work?

Unit 2 Final task: Working together

What?	Work as a group to research and present findings.
	Choose a topic from the ideas map.
	Create a bar chart, a pictogram or a table.
	Develop a presentation about the topic.
How?	Work in groups of 4 or 5.
	Make sure every group member has a job to do.

What can you do to be successful in this task? Listen to your teacher.

Success means ...
We understood the topic.
Everyone had a role to play.
We used the information we collected in this unit.
We represented our findings in a bar chart, a pictogram or a table.
Our presentation was well-organised and interesting.

1 Choose a topic and understand the task.

Discuss what needs to be done in your group.

- What information do you already have?
- Do you need to collect more data?
- How will you present your final report?
- Will you use a pictogram, a bar chart, or words and pictures in your report?
- Who will be responsible for each part of the task?

 **2**  **Work in your group.**

Ideas map

at home

at play

at work

at school

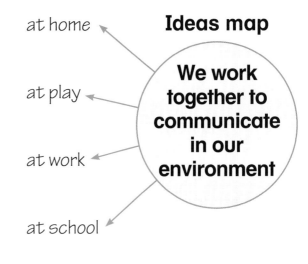

We work together to communicate in our environment

Researcher: to find any extra information you need about your topic.

Information checker: to be in charge of checking and organising information.

Recorders: to work on the bar chart, pictogram or table.

Presenters: to practise what they will say when they do the presentation.

Checklist for the group
- Have you used your worksheets as a source of data?
- Do you have any extra information that you need?
- Has all the data been carefully counted and recorded?
- Is the information clear on your bar chart, pictogram or table?
- Do you have a conclusion about what the data means?

3 **Present your research findings.**

- Introduce each member of the group.
- Let each person say what part of the task they were responsible for.
- Then let the presenters give the presentation.
- Take questions form the audience after the presentation.

Reflection: How well did you work together

a 👥 💬 Discuss the task in your group.

Final task checklist			
Did everyone have a role to play?	😊	😐	☹️
Did we share information that we collected from earlier lessons?	😊	😐	☹️
Was our presentation well organised?	😊	😐	☹️

b 👤 ✏️ Complete the worksheet.

c 👥 💬 What did you learn about working together?

- Did you enjoy working in your group?
- What could you have done differently?
- What did you learn about how teams work?

Before you go

- If you did another group presentation in the future, which role in the team would you like to take?

Unit 3 How do we keep safe?

What do you know?
- How can we keep safe in our homes?
- How can we get to school safely?
- Dangers! How do we know about them?
- Who can tell us about local dangers?
- How do we know if food is safe to eat?
- How can we be safe online?

In this unit, you will:
- find out more about how to keep safe
- present a safety idea to the class and explain where you got your information from.

3.1 How can we keep safe in our homes?

1 👥 💬 **What makes you feel safe?**

2 👥 💬 **What do you think each sign means?**

- Where would you see each sign?
- What other signs do you see at home?

A

B

C

FRAGILE

D

⚠ **CAUTION**

**Hot Surface.
Do NOT touch.**

Allow to cool before servicing.

E

CAUTION

WET FLOOR

F

0–3

⚠ **WARNING:**

CHOKING HAZARD — Small parts not for children under 3 years, or any individuals who have a tendency to place inedible objects into their mouths.

3 😃 💬 **Give reasons for your opinions about the signs.**

4 😃 💬 **Look at the pictures below.**

- What does each sign say?
- Which sign is useful in a home? Give a reason.

5 😃 💬 ✏️ **Look at the pictures on your worksheet. Discuss whether they show things that are safe or dangerous.**

How could you make them safer? Complete the worksheet.

6 😃 💬 **Present your ideas to the class.**

- Give your opinion about why something is dangerous.
- Show and explain what you will do to make it safer.

> **Useful language**
>
> To give a reason, use words like: *because, so that, that is why.*

> **Key term**
>
> **opinion:** a thought or belief about something, which cannot be proved to be true or false

> **Before you go**
>
> - What else can you do to make everyone safer at home?

> **Talking point**
>
> - What have you learned about safety signs at home?

3.2 How can we get to school safely?

1 👥 💬 **Are these safe ways to get to school? Give your opinion, with a reason.**

2 👤 👥 ✏️ **Complete the worksheet, giving your opinions.**

3 👥 💬 **Talk with a partner about getting to school safely.**

Is it safe to cross the river?

No. The water is high.

That's a problem. What can we do?

We can hold hands and walk slowly.

4 👥 💬 **Share your ideas about how to help with problems getting to school safely.**

Talking point

- What idea did you share about getting to school safely? Can your classmates use this idea?

Before you go

- How else can you travel safely?

3.3 Dangers! How do we know about them?

✓ Collaboration
✓ Evaluation
✓ Communication

1 😯 💬 **Which pictures give warnings?**

- What do the **warnings** mean?
- Where might you see them?

Key term

warnings: something that is written or said to tell people about possible dangers

2 👥 💬 **What do we do if there is a fire?**

ASSEMBLY POINT

3 👥 ✏️ **Make a fire drill plan for your class. Use the worksheet.**

4 👥 💬 **Present your fire drill to the class and discuss it. Answer questions from the class.**

Talking point

- How well did you work in a group to make and present the fire drill plan?

Before you go

- When might we get warnings? Who might give a warning?

3.4 Who can tell us about local dangers?

1 👥 💬 **Look at the pictures and answer the questions.**

- Do you know these plants and animals?
- Do you think any of them are dangerous? Why?
- How could you find out?

2 👥 💬 **How can you find out about dangerous plants and animals where you live?**

- What information do you need to find out?
- Who can you ask?
- What questions should you ask?

3 👥 ✏️ **Write questions to find out about dangerous plants or animals. Use the worksheet.**

4 👤 ✏️ **Carry out your research. Record your answers on the worksheet.**

5 👥 💬 **Tell the class what you found out.**

Useful language

You can ask questions in different ways. For example:

Is that plant poisonous?

Where does it grow?

Do you know anything about this animal? Does it bite?

How do you know?

Talking point

- What did you do to help with this investigation?

Before you go

- What else would you like to know about dangerous plants and animals? How could you find out?

3.5 How do we know if food is safe to eat?

1 👥 📖 **What can a story tell us?**

Read the story and answer the questions.

* What is the story about?
* Can you learn about food safety from this story? If so, what?
* What will you remember about this story?

1

Jo ate some fish.

2

Now she feels sick.

3

I will be more careful this time.

4

That's better!

2 👥 💬 **Talk about any bad experiences you have had with food.**

* What made you sick?
* Why?

3 🗫 💬 **Look at the poster and answer the questions.**

- Is this poster a good **source** of information about food safety?
- What information does it give us?
- How does it help us to understand and remember information?

Key term

source: the person, place or thing, that you get information from

FOOD SAFETY

Wash your hands

Wash fruit and vegetables

Keep food fresh

Cover cooked food

Be careful

4 🗫 ✏️ **Make up a short story to teach others about food safety. Use the worksheet to plan the story.**

Talking point

- Did you find the story or the poster the most interesting?

Before you go

- Where else can we find information about food safety?

3.6 How can we be safe online?

1 👥 📖 **Read what people say about finding information online.**

A — You can get a lot of good information online.

B — Yes, but you have to be careful!

C — And be nice to people online. Don't bully!

D — But be careful who you talk to!

E — And be careful what you click on!

F — Just have fun!

2 👥 📖 💬 **Read and discuss the poster.**

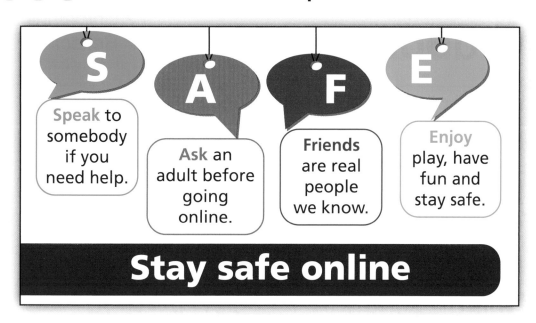

3 👥 💬 **What can go wrong if you are not careful online?**

- Can bad things happen? What can happen?
- Can others get hurt?

4 👥 💬 **What can you do to stay safe?**

a Discuss this question in groups.

b Draw up a list of online safety tips with your teacher.

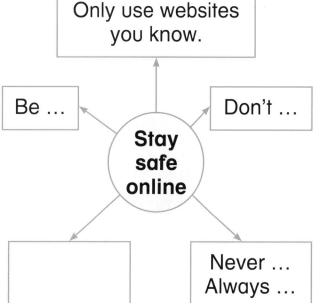

Talking point

- Where can you find sources of information?

Before you go

- Are online sources of information more useful than other sources?

Unit 3 Final task: Talk about safety

What?	Tell others about a safety idea that you think is important.
	Talk about why you have used a picture, story, poster or warning sign to show your idea.
How?	Work in groups.
	Use a story, a picture, a poster, or a warning sign to show your safety idea.

What can you do to be successful in this task? Listen to your teacher.

Success means …
We have told others about a good safety idea.
We were able to make others understand the idea.
We were able to explain why we used a story, picture, poster or warning sign to show our idea.

1 **Look at some of the safety ideas you have talked about in this unit.**

- Look at the sources you have used in this unit, which presented safety ideas.
- Make notes on the chart. Use the worksheet.

Safety idea	How information is presented (poster, sign, etc.)
....	**1** .... Why is this way of presenting the information useful? ....
....	**2** .... Why is this way of presenting the information useful? ....

2 🙁 💬 **Discuss your presentation. Which safety idea would you like to present to others? Why do you think it is important?**

- What can you do to present this idea? Will you use a sign, a poster, a story or a picture?
- What will you need to make your presentation?

3 🙁 ✏️ **Prepare your presentation.**

- Who will do each task?
- How and when will you practise your presentation?

4 🙁 💬 **Present your ideas to the class.**

- Be prepared to answer some questions about your ideas.

5 🙁 💬 **Discuss the presentations.**

- Were the safety tips useful?
- Were they presented in a way that helps you to remember them?

Reflection: How did you contribute to the presentation?

a 👥 💬 Discuss the task in your group.

Final task checklist			
Did you present a useful safety idea?	☺	😐	☹
Were you able to make others understand your idea?	☺	😐	☹
Were you able to explain why you used a story, a picture, a sign or a poster?	☺	😐	☹
Did you answer questions about the presentation?	☺	😐	☹

b 👤 ✏ Complete the worksheet.

c 👥 💬 Think about the other presentations.
   • What did you learn from them?
   • Which presentation did you enjoy the most? Why?

Before you go

• What is the most important thing you have learned in this unit?
• What more would you like to find out about staying safe?
• Who could you ask?

Unit 4 One step at a time

What do you know?

- How is planet Earth?
- What is happening underwater?
- How do we find out about life in water?
- What is happening on land?
- How can weather affect life on land?
- How can we help planet Earth?

In this unit, you will:

- find out about different forms of information
- discover what you know and what other people know
- understand that different people know different things
- suggest a personal action that could help planet Earth.

4.1 How is planet Earth?

1 👥 💬 **Talk about these photographs.**

- Say what you think is happening in each set of photographs.
- What do you know about what is happening in these photographs?
- How do you know this?
- What do your classmates think?
- What do your classmates know about what is happening?

clean water

making water dirty

a forest

cutting down trees

2 👥 💬 **Look at the list of problems on planet Earth.**

- Discuss the problems with your partner.
- Tell each other which problems you know about.
- Are there any problems that you, and your partner, can add to the list?

3 👥 💬 ✏️ **What might be a problem in your community?**

- Do you think your community has any problems like the ones in Activity 2?
- Take turns to talk about a problem that can damage your environment.
- Why are there problems? Take turns to talk about what you think is the reason for each problem.
- Use the worksheet to write down your ideas.

Talking point

- What different ideas did your group have?

Before you go

- Were you able to say what was a problem in your community? What ideas do you have to solve the problem?

Pollution

1) Litter
2) Car fumes
3) Oil spills
4) Factory smoke

5) **Rubbish**
6) **Waste** going into ponds, rivers, lakes and the ocean
7) Cutting down too many trees

Key terms

pollution: poisonous or dirty substances that are polluting water, air or land

rubbish: unwanted things or waste material such as used paper, empty bottles and waste food

waste: things that have been used and are no longer wanted

4.2 What is happening underwater?

1 👥 💬 **Look at the different types of information.**

• Discuss the questions under each picture.

A

• **What does the picture show?**
• **What information does it give you?**

B

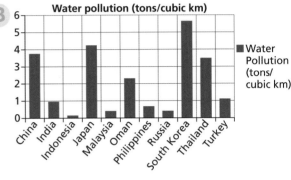

• **What kind of graph is this?**
• **What information does it show you?**
• **Which countries show the highest measurements of pollution on the graph?**

C

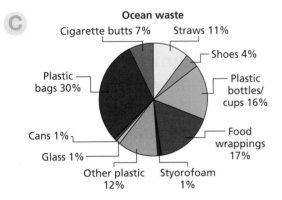

• **Why do you think this is called a 'pie chart'?**
• **What is most of the rubbish in our oceans made of?**
• **What other rubbish is in our oceans?**

D

• **What does this photograph show?**
• **Where do you think the photographer is?**

2 👥 💬 **Discuss these questions with your partner.**

- What is the same about pictures A to D on page 52?

- What kind of pollution is there in water, according to pictures A to D?

- Which picture do you think is the most useful? Tell your partner why.

Find out more about water pollution on the internet.

3 👥 💬 **What do you know?**

- Use the worksheet to identify the causes of water pollution.

- Choose two sources to discuss with your partner.

- Let your partner explain two sources to you, and give their opinion about how to solve the problem.

Talking point

- What new ways of showing information have you learned about?

Before you go

- Which way of showing information would you choose if you were making a presentation? Give a reason for your answer.

4.3 How can we find out about life in water?

1 🎎 📖 **Read this story, 'The Pond'.**

1 We went on a field trip. Jack had a magnifying glass. Mari took notes and Jane took photographs.

2 We saw frogs and dragonflies at the pond. Jack had never seen a dragonfly before!

3 We saw a lot of fish. Can you count how many?

4 Then a heron came and frightened the fish away. Herons love to eat fish!

- What kind of information were the children looking for?
- What tools did they have to help them find the information?
- How did they collect the information and record it?

54

2 👥 ✏️ Go on a field trip.

- **Plan your trip.**
  - Who will count the things you find?
  - Who will write down the information?
  - What equipment do you need to take with you?

- **Discuss the information you need to find.**
  - What examples of living things are you looking for?
  - What fish or other creatures might you find?
  - Will you also count plants?
  - What examples of water pollution are you looking for?
- **Do your research.**
- **Record your findings on the worksheet.**

3 👥 💬 Talk about your findings.

- What living things, creatures and plants did you find?
- What examples of water pollution did you see?

Compare in your group how many of each thing you found.

4 👥 💬 How do people affect life in water?

- What affects life in water in your community?
- How have people made this problem happen?
- What can we do to make things better?
- Can you think of an invention to help with the problem?

Talking point
- What was challenging about this task?

Before you go
- What can you do to help life in water in the future?

4.4 What is happening on land?

1 👥 💬 **Look at the different pictures.**

- What do pictures A to D have in common?
- What information, or message, does each picture give you?

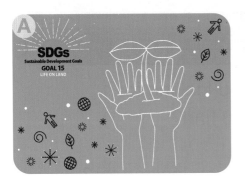

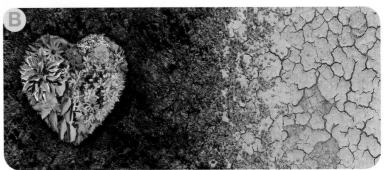

2 👥 💬 **Discuss these questions with your partner.**

- Picture A: What do you think the two hands holding the plant mean?
- Picture B: Complete this sentence: *If we don't love and look after plants …*
- Picture C: What do the lungs represent? Why are they so important to us?
- Picture D: What are the three reasons why people cut down trees?
- Which picture do you think gives the best information? Explain why to your partner.

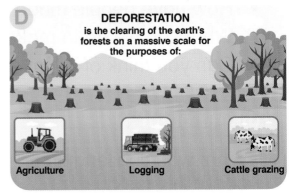

3 👥 ✏️ 💬 **Write a question and talk about the issues.**

Read about **deforestation** and **desertification** in the Useful language box. Choose one.

- Write a question about it.
- Swap your question with another pair.
- Write down the answer to their question.

4 👥 ✏️ **Find out more. Choose a picture from A to D on page 56.**

- On the worksheet, write down all the information you can get from the picture. How can you find out more?
- You can ask the librarian to show you books at the library. Look for books about deserts and forests.
- You can ask an adult to help you find information on the internet. Search for the words in the Useful language box.

Write at least three new things that you have learned.

Useful language

deforestation: when trees in forests are cut down and not replanted

desertification: when fertile land becomes a desert. This means that land has become so dry that people no longer grow plants or keep animals there. It usually happens because of drought, deforestation, or too much farming.

Talking point

- What new information did you find? Where did you find the information?

Before you go

- Do you think infographics are a good way of presenting information? Explain why, or why not.

4.5 How can weather affect life on land?

✓ Analysis
✓ Communication

1 👥 📖 **Read this story and answer the questions.**

Mrs Goh is a lettuce farmer. When she started farming, she grew her lettuces in her field. The sun shone on the lettuces and the rain watered them. She sold her lettuces at the market.

Then there was a drought. No rain fell. The sun was so hot that it dried up the lettuces. Mrs Goh had to think of a new plan.

Her neighbours helped her to build a greenhouse. She planted new lettuces in the greenhouse. The greenhouse protected the lettuces from the sun. Mrs Goh watered the plants from a well that the villagers dug.

Now she has new lettuces. She gives some lettuces to her neighbours every day and takes the rest to the market.

Discuss these questions in class.

- How did Mrs Goh farm in the beginning?
- Why did she have to change the way she farmed?
- What did she do to protect her lettuces?
- Where did she get water from?
- What is her life like now?

2 👥 💬 **How else can weather affect the land? Discuss other kinds of weather.**

- What happens if it rains too much?
- What can happen in very strong winds?
- Have you experienced very bad weather?

3 👥 💬 **What can you do to help if the weather causes problems on land in your community?**

- Discuss ideas with your partner. Use the ideas map and the photographs to help you.

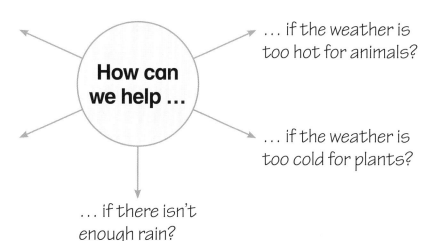

... if the weather is too hot for plants?

... if the weather is too hot for animals?

How can we help ...

... if the weather is too cold for animals?

... if the weather is too cold for plants?

... if there isn't enough rain?

Talking point

- Was it difficult to think about ways you can help?

Before you go

- Which idea did you find the most interesting? Do you think it could help in your community?

4.6 How can we help planet Earth?

1 👥 💬 **What problem can we help with?**

Choose one of the ideas that you talked about with your partner in the last lesson and explain it to your group. Tell them:

- the weather problem
- how your idea can help with the problem.

Listen to each other and ask questions to make sure you understand each person's idea.

2 👥 **What will we do?**

Decide on the weather problem that your group would like to help with. Try to think of a clever invention that your group could design to help solve this problem.

You can use ideas that you talked about in the last lesson. Look at these pictures to help you.

Could we make something to protect plants?

Could we collect rainwater? How would we use it?

Could we help to provide shade for animals?

3 👥 💬 **With your group, decide on the invention that you would like to illustrate in the next lesson. Talk about how your idea would work. Use the worksheet.**

Invention:
- What would it be used for?
- What materials would you need to make it?
- How would it work?
- What would each person in the group do?
- Would you need help from adults?
- What steps would you need to take to make the invention?

4 👤 ✏️ **What is your role?**

- What part did you play in deciding on which weather problem to choose?
- What part did you play in thinking of an invention to help with the weather problem?

Talking point

- Was it easy for your group to decide which weather problem to help with?

Before you go

- Share your idea with another group. Ask if they have any suggestions for adding to it before you present it.

Unit 4 Final task: Helping planet Earth

✓ **Collaboration**
✓ Communication
✓ Reflection

What?	Draw your idea for helping with a problem caused by weather.
	Say what the problem is.
	Explain how your idea could help with the problem.
How?	Work in groups of 4 or 5.
	Present your idea and listen to the ideas presented by other groups.

What can you do to be successful in this task? Listen to your teacher.

Success means ...
We explained our idea clearly.
We answered questions.
Everyone in our group had a role to play.

1 Prepare for the task.

- Has your group decided how to help with a problem caused by weather?
- Talk about how you could illustrate your idea.
- Talk about how you will present your idea.
- Decide what each person in your group will do to illlustrate and present your idea.

2 🫂 **On a large sheet of paper, draw your idea.**

Checklist

✓ Decide what each person in your group will do.
✓ Give the invention a name.
✓ Draw the invention.
✓ Add labels to explain how it's made.
✓ Add captions to explain how it's used.

3 🫂 **Present your group's idea to the class.**

- Decide what part everyone will play in the presentation.
- Tell the class about the weather problem your group has chosen.
- Explain how your idea would help with this problem.
- Take questions from the audience after the presentation.

4 **Find out more about the ideas that your classmates have suggested.**

- Listen to your classmates explain their ideas.
- Ask questions to find out more about their ideas.

5 **Let the audience vote for the top three ideas.**

After everyone has had a chance to do their presentation:
- Your teacher will ask for a show of hands.
- Vote for the idea that you think is the best.
- Be prepared to say why you believe this is the best idea.

Reflection: How well did we work together?

a  Discuss the task in your group.

Final task checklist			
Did our team work well together?	☺	😐	☹
Did everyone in our group have a role to play?	☺	😐	☹
Were we able to explain our plan clearly?	☺	😐	☹
Was the information we provided useful?	☺	😐	☹

b Complete the worksheet.

Before you go

- How can you put your plans into action?
- Choose three plans that your class can put into action.
- Follow through on these plans.

Unit **5** Which activities are good for us?

What do you know?

- How can we keep healthy?
- How fast do we breathe?
- How fast do our hearts beat?
- Can our heart and breathing rates change?
- How do we record findings?

- What other sources of information can we use?

In this unit, you will:

- talk about what happens to your heart and lungs when you exercise
- make a poster, which shows your opinions about the benefits of exercise.

5.1 How can we keep healthy?

1 👥 💬 **Listen to the speaker talking about exercise. Ask questions.**

> What can I do to be healthy?

> How do I know if I am healthy?

2 👥 📖 **Read the information on the next page.**

> Where are our lungs and our heart?

> What do they do?

3 👥 📖 💬 **Ask and answer questions.**

Read the text again. Ask your partner questions about the text. For example:

- What does your heart do?
- What do we breathe in and out?

4 👤 ✏️ **What else do you want to find out about? Write questions to use in your research. Use the worksheet.**

> How do you know that your heart is beating?

> What happens when you run?

Talking point

- What did you learn in this lesson?

Before you go

- How can we find out more about the heart and lungs?

66

Is exercise important?

How can we be healthy? We know that our body needs food, water and sleep. But what about exercise?

What happens when we exercise?

We have organs inside our body called the heart and the lungs.

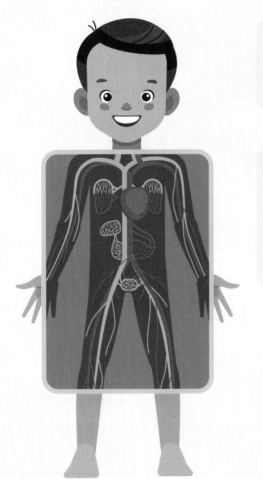

The heart pumps blood to all parts of the body.

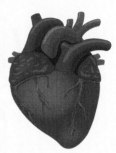

We have two lungs, which help us to breathe in and out.

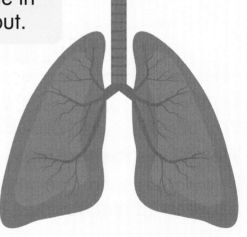

The heart pumps blood around our body.
Blood carries nutrients (food) and oxygen to parts of our body.
Blood also helps to remove that things our body does not need.

Lungs help us to breathe. We breathe in oxygen (air) that we need and we breathe out air that we don't need.

Exercise makes these organs work harder.
This extra work helps to keep us healthy.

5.2 How fast do we breathe?

1 👥 📖 **Read the information about breathing.**

Breathing

You breathe in and out all day and night.
We call this **respiration**.
If you are resting, you will breathe in and out between 18 and 30 times in one minute.

Key term
respiration: breathing

2 👥 📖 **How can you measure your breathing rate?**

a Watch a demonstration.
b Read the instructions.
- Put your hands on your chest.
- Feel your chest go out as you breathe in.
- Feel your chest go in as you breathe out.
- Count your breaths in and out. In + out = one breath.

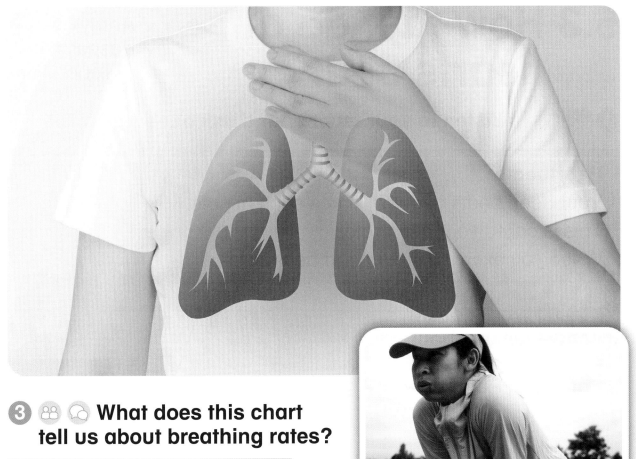

3 👥 💬 **What does this chart tell us about breathing rates?**

Name	Breaths per minute
Anya	~~||||~~ ~~||||~~ ~~||||~~ ~~||||~~
Po	~~||||~~ ~~||||~~ ~~||||~~ ~~||||~~ ~~||||~~
Tim	~~||||~~ ~~||||~~ ~~||||~~ ~~||||~~ ||

4 👥 ✏️ **What are your breathing rates?**

a Count the number of times your partner breathes in and out.

b Record the information on the worksheet.

c Share your information with others.

Talking point

- What did you learn about your breathing?

Before you go

- What else do you think you could measure?

5.3 How fast do our hearts beat?

1 👥 📖 💬 **Listen to your teacher and ask questions.**

Heartbeats

Your heart beats about 70 times each minute.
This is called your heart rate.
When you exercise, your heart beats faster!

2 👥 📖 **What does this chart tell us about the heart rates of Anya, Po and Tim?**

Tips

- Read the title and any captions first.
- Count in tens to read the numbers.

Heartbeats per minute

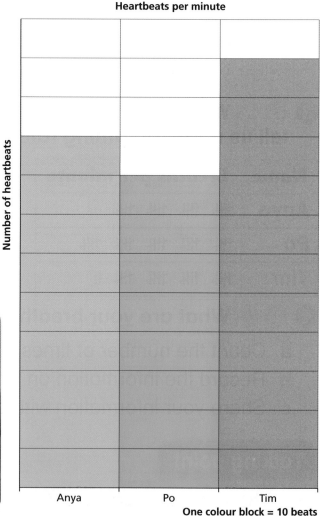

Number of heartbeats

Anya   Po   Tim

One colour block = 10 beats

3 👥 💬 **How can you measure your heart rate? Watch a demonstration.**

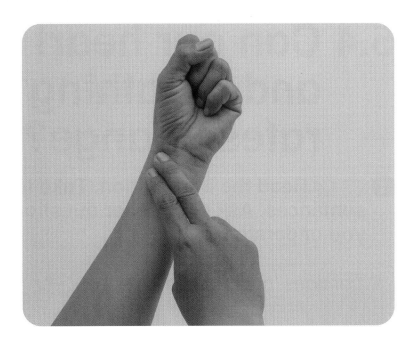

- Put your fingers on the pulse. Can you feel the heartbeats?
- Listen to your teacher. Count the heartbeats quietly.

4 👥 ✏️ **What is your heart rate? With a partner, count your heartbeats.**

- Count your heartbeats.
- Record the information on the worksheet.
- Share your information with others.

Talking point

- What did you learn about your heart?

Before you go

- Can you measure your heart rate in a different way?
- Can your heart and breathing rates change? How?

5.4 Can our heart and breathing rates change?

1 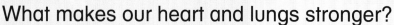 📖 **Read the information. Take turns to read the sentences. Ask each other questions to make sure you understand.**

What does 'out of breath' mean?

How do you know that your heart and lungs are working harder?

What makes our heart and lungs stronger?

Heart and breathing rates

Do you feel tired and hot after exercise? Do you feel 'out of breath' and thirsty? That means your heart and lungs are working harder. Our heart and lungs become stronger when we exercise.

2 😊 💬 **Discuss how you can do an investigation into changes to our heart or breathing rates.**

- What shall we test?
- When shall we test?
- How will we record data?
- What will we need?

Useful language

In an **investigation**, we try to find the answer to a question. We may think we know the answer and so we **predict** the answer. Then we take measurements and record the results (**data**).

3 😁 ✏️ **Prepare an investigation.**

  a Read the questions below with your teacher.

  b Complete the worksheet.

1 What will you investigate? Write down the question you will ask.
2 What do you **predict** will happen?
3 What will you do? Describe the procedure.

Key term

predict: when you say what you think will happen

4 😁 💬 **Tell another pair about what you are going to investigate and how you will do it. Use the information from your worksheet.**

Talking point

• What did you do to help another pair with their investigation?

Before you go

• What else do you need to prepare before the investigation?

5.5 How do we record findings?

✓ Research
✓ Collaboration

1 👥 💬 **Talk about how to do the investigation.**

- Will you measure heart rates or breathing rates?
- What will you do to make this a fair test?

2 👥 💬 **Look at the tally chart and discuss what information you will need to complete it.**

- Where will you write your name?
- What will you have to do to get the information?
- Who will count and who will record first?

.... rate per minute

Name	Resting	After exercise
	~~HH~~ ~~HH~~ . . . ____ + ____ = ____ per minute	~~HH~~ ~~HH~~ . . . ____ + ____ = ____ per minute
	~~HH~~ ~~HH~~ . . . ____ + ____ = ____ per minute	~~HH~~ ~~HH~~ . . . ____ + ____ = ____ per minute

> **Remember:** You can measure the rate for 30 seconds and then add the numbers.

3 🤝 ✏️ **Carry out your investigation and record your findings on the worksheet.**

4 👥 💬 **Discuss your findings. What did you find out?**

- Were the two rates the same?
- Was one rate higher than the other? Which one was higher?
- What does this mean?

Talking point

- What did you learn about working with others?

Before you go

- If you did this investigation again, what would you do differently?

5.6 What other sources of information can we use?

1 What are these sources of information about?

A

B

C

| Makes you stronger |

| Makes you sleep well | Makes you feel happy |

Why exercise is good for you

It's fun!

Gives you energy

D

Answers to the question: Who do you exercise with?			
	My family	My friends	My team
Priti	✓		
Sam		✓	✓
Anna	✓	✓	✓
Tsepo	✓		
Ashraf			✓

2 🗣 💬 **Discuss these questions about sources A to D.**

a What does the photograph (A) tell you about exercise?

b Which source gives ideas about exercise? Which ideas do you like?

c What information does the ideas map (C) give you?

d What question did Priti, Sam, Anna, Tsepo and Ashraf answer (D)?

e Which source is the most interesting and useful? Why?

f What other sources of information could you use?

3 🗣 💬 **With your teacher, talk about:**

• the four sources of information in Activity 1

• the research you have done in previous lessons.

4 🗣 ✏️ **How can you show what you have learned on a poster?**

Follow these steps and record your answers on the worksheet.

1 Talk about the information in this unit. What did you find the most interesting?

2 Which ideas would you like to present on a poster? Which sources will you need?

3 Start collecting information from different sources to make a poster.

> I learned about how my heart rate changes.

> I learned how to ask good questions!

Talking point

• What have you learned about finding information in different sources?

Before you go

• What other sources would you like to use?

Unit 5 Final task: Make a poster about exercise

| ✓ **Collaboration** |
| ✓ Communication |
| ✓ Reflection |

What?	Make a poster that shows your ideas about why exercise is good for us.
	Present your ideas to the class, using the poster.
How?	Work in teams. Each team member should have a clear role.
	Use sources you have made during the lessons.
	Present them on your poster.

What can you do to be successful in this task? Listen to your teacher.

Success means …
We have worked together to share ideas and make a good poster.
We each had a role, and we all made a contribution to the task.
We were able to make others understand our ideas.

1 👥 💬 **Discuss the information you have collected so far and what you want to present.**

- What will your poster be about?
- What sources do you already have?
- Do you have three ideas to present on your poster?
- How will you show these ideas? For example: pictures, diagrams, charts, stories.
- Do you need any extra information? If so, which sources will you use?

② 👥 💬 Discuss the presentation and your roles.

- How will you make your poster: on paper or on a screen?
- Do you have everything you need to do this?
- Can you share resources with other groups?
- How will everyone help? Each person in the team should have a role to play.

③ 👥 ✏️ Plan your poster.

- Look at the plan below first and discuss it with your team.
- Use the worksheet to help you plan your poster.
- Make a rough draft of your poster.

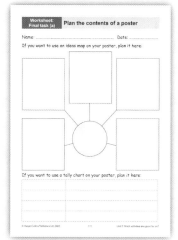

④ 👥 ✏️ Make your poster.

- Remember to fill in the space on the poster.
- Use colours and large print so others can read it easily.

⑤ 👥 💬 Present your poster to the class. Follow these steps.

1 State your ideas.
2 Talk about the sources of information you used to support your ideas.
- Did you use your own research? Explain what you did.
- Did you use other sources? Name the sources.
3 End with a short conclusion and state your ideas again.

Reflection: How successful was your poster?

a 👥 💬 Discuss the task in your group.

Final task checklist			
Did you all help to make the poster?	😊	😐	🙁
Did you listen to each other and discuss the ideas?	😊	😐	🙁
Did you use different sources of information to support your ideas?	😊	😐	🙁
Did the other groups find your presentation interesting?	😊	😐	🙁

b 🧑 ✏️ Complete the worksheet.

c 👥 💬 Discuss the presentations with your teacher.
- Which presentations worked well?
- Why did they work well?
- What could your group have done differently?

Before you go

- What else would you like to find out about physical activities?

Glossary

app: a program with a picture on a phone, tablet or computer, which allows you to do special things

bar chart: a graph that uses rectangular shapes to represent the size or amount of something

community: a group of people who live in a particular place, or who are similar in some way

data: information, especially when it is in the form of facts or statistics (numbers)

deforestation: when trees in forests are cut down and not replanted

desertification: when fertile land becomes a desert; this means that land has become so dry that people can no longer grow plants or animals there

device: something that is mechanical or electrical (such as a phone or a television) that we use for a particular purpose

ideas map: a graphic diagram to help us show and sort out ideas

investigation: the process of trying to find out what has happened, or what is the truth

litter: rubbish that is left lying around outside

pictogram: a simple drawing that represents something

pollution: poisonous or dirty substances that are polluting water, air or land

predict: when you say what you think will happen

problem: a situation that causes difficulties

respiration: breathing

rubbish: unwanted things or waste material such as used paper, empty bottles and waste food

screen: the flat part of a device on which you can read and see things

solution: a way of dealing with a problem or difficulty

source: the person, place or thing, that you get information from

technology: the use of knowledge to invent new devices or tools

warnings: something that is written or said to tell people about possible dangers

waste: things that have been used and are no longer wanted

Acknowledgements

The publishers gratefully acknowledge the permission granted to reproduce copyright material in this book. Every effort has been made to trace copyright holders and to obtain their permission for the use of copyright material. The publishers will gladly receive any information enabling them to rectify any error or omission at the first opportunity. The publishers would like to thank the following for permission to reproduce copyright material:

Cover and title page tamu1500/Shutterstock, p.1 LightField Studios/Shutterstock, p.2 Aimee and the Tablet, Text and Illustrations © HarperCollinsPublishers Limited 2020, p.3 Martial Red/Shutterstock, p.3 New Africa/Shutterstock, p.3 Hananeko_Studio/ Shutterstock, p.4 Sunnydream/Shutterstock, p.4 z576/Shutterstock, p.4 Olga_Lots/Shutterstock, p.4 Morphart Creation/ Shutterstock, p.4 fullvector/Shutterstock, p.4 McLittle Stock/Shutterstock, p.8 Patrick Foto/Shutterstock, p.8 MNStudio/Shutterstock, p.8 TinnaPong/Shutterstock, p.8 Prostock-studio/Shutterstock, p.8 fizkes/Shutterstock, p.9 Sim Lev/Shutterstock, p.10 Ground Picture/Shutterstock, p.10 BearFotos/Shutterstock, p.10 namtipStudio/Shutterstock, p.11 niroworld/Shutterstock, p.12 Art Alex/ Shutterstock, p.12 Lukmanazis/Shutterstock, p.13 gomolach/Shutterstock, p.13 MiniDoodle/Shutterstock, p.13 5 second Studio/ Shutterstock, p.13 Nearbirds/Shutterstock, p.14 vectorfusionart/Shutterstock, p.15 Red Fox studio/Shutterstock, p.15 ImageNavi on OFFSET/Shutterstock, p.17 ebonyeg/Shutterstock, p.19 Look Studio/Shutterstock, p.19 wavebreakmedia/Shutterstock, p.20 KanKhem/Shutterstock, p.21 Daria Nipot/Shutterstock, p.21 VH-studio/Shutterstock, p.21 Blue Planet Studio/Shutterstock, p.21 Johnny Habell/Shutterstock, p.23 Ground Picture/Shutterstock, p.24 Evgeniy Kalinovskiy/Shutterstock, p.24 ziggy_mars/ Shutterstock, p.24 Fotokostic/Shutterstock, p.24 KPG-Payless/Shutterstock, p.26 Passakorn Umpornmaha/Shutterstock, p.26 infinetsoft/Shutterstock, p.26 Zoart Studio/Shutterstock, p.26 mushan/Shutterstock, p.26 TotemArt/Shutterstock, p.26 MisterEmil/Shutterstock, p.26 infinetsoft/Shutterstock, p.27 MIA Studio/Shutterstock, p.27 Brandon Bourdages/Shutterstock, p.28 Stock-Asso/Shutterstock, p.28 chali_studio/Shutterstock, p.28 JU.STOCKER/Shutterstock, p.28 goodmoments/Shutterstock, p.29 wavebreakmedia/Shutterstock, p.30 Ihor Bulyhin/Shutterstock, p.32 chuck hsu/Shutterstock, p.33 Jaroslav Machacek/ Shutterstock, p.34 Adisak Panongram/Shutterstock, p.34 Viktorija Reuta/Shutterstock, p.34 sweeann/Shutterstock, p.34 ARSbright/ Shutterstock, p.34 Mironov Konstantin/Shutterstock, p.34 Sudowoodo/Shutterstock, p.35 Pretty Vectors/Shutterstock, p.35 Flat vectors/Shutterstock, p.35 Giles Kent/Shutterstock, p.36 Noey smiley/Shutterstock, p.36 d13/Shutterstock, p.36 Ann in the uk/ Shutterstock, p.36 Irina Wilhauk/Shutterstock, p.36 Sergey Novikov/Shutterstock, p.36 R_Boe/Shutterstock, p.37 Arief Budi Kusuma/Shutterstock, p.38 teera.noisakran/Shutterstock, p.38 aleksandr Naim/Shutterstock, p.38 Anton Prohorov/Shutterstock, p.38 VECTORWORKS_ENTERPRISE/Shutterstock, p.38 KK_face/Shutterstock, p.38 siarifzen/Shutterstock, p.38 StudioFI/Shutterstock, p.38 vali.lung/Shutterstock, p.39 Pix One/Shutterstock, p.39 Anastasia Averina/Shutterstock, p.39 I AM A CREATOR/Shutterstock, p.39 BNP Design Studio/Shutterstock, p.40 nilsmen/Shutterstock, p.40 teekayu/Shutterstock, p.40 FotoLot/Shutterstock, p.40 nico99/Shutterstock, p.40 yod 67/Shutterstock, p.40 Klaus Ulrich Mueller/Shutterstock, p.40 Mauro Rodrigues/Shutterstock, p.41 Katy FosterShutterstock, p.44 Nadya_Art/Shutterstock, p.44 Nadya_Art/Shutterstock, p.44 fizkes/Shutterstock, p.46 Oleksandr Chukhil/Shutterstock, p.46 jittawit21/Shutterstock, p.46 Rawpixel.com/Shutterstock, p.50 Rocksweeper/Shutterstock, p.50 Vladislav Gajic/Shutterstock, p.50 urioso.Photography/Shutterstock, p.50 Rich Carey/Shutterstock, p.51 Haris120297/Shutterstock, p.52 RURI BYAKU/Shutterstock, p.52 GreenOak/Shutterstock, p.54 The Pond, ©HarperCollinsPublishers Limited 2005, p.55 Sue Robinson/ Shutterstock, p.56 RURI BYAKU/Shutterstock, p.56 Lightspring/Shutterstock, p.56 Myroshnichenko Violetta/Shutterstock, p.57 PARALAXIS/Shutterstock, p.57 ArCaLu/Shutterstock, p.58 pornpawit/Shutterstock, p.58 Alexander Raths/Shutterstock , p.58 Emine Kamaci/Shutterstock, p.59 narikan/Shutterstock, p.59 Mulevich/Shutterstock, p.59 grafxart/Shutterstock, p.60 Stella_E/ Shutterstock, p.60 Evelyn Joubert/Shutterstock, p.60 EvrenDumanoglu/Shutterstock, p.60 Dina Gomankova/Shutterstock, p.60 Lea Rae/Shutterstock, p.60 larisa Stefanjuk/Shutterstock, p.60 goodmoments/Shutterstock, p.60 Couanon Julien/Shutterstock, p.62 udra11/Shutterstock, p.63 latas/Shutterstock, p.64 onShore/Shutterstock, p.64 EvgeniiAnd/Shutterstock, p.65 Monkey Business Images/Shutterstock, p.66 BAZA Production/Shutterstock, p.67 Bahau/Shutterstock, p.67 digitmilk/Shutterstock, p.67 Lucia Fox/ Shutterstock, p.68 Natewimon Nantiwat/Shutterstock, p.69 Orawan Pattarawimonchai/Shutterstock, p.69 T.Photo/Shutterstock, p.70 izkes/Shutterstock, p.71 Phuangphech/Shutterstock, p.71 Xolodan/Shutterstock, p.71 SeventyFour/Shutterstock, p.72 Colorfuel Studio/Shutterstock, p.73 Sergey Nivens/Shutterstock, p.74 dragon_fang/Shutterstock, p.74 Ground Picture/Shutterstock, p.75 wavebreakmedia/Shutterstock, p.76 WoodysPhotos/Shutterstock, p.76 toyotoyo/Shutterstock, p.78 Sergey Novikov/ Shutterstock, p.79 NataSnow/Shutterstock, p.80 TinnaPong/Shutterstock

Definitions adapted from Collins Cobuild Dictionary.